# WHAT WE FACE WALKING OUT THE FRONT DOOR

*WHAT WE FACE
WALKING
OUT
THE
FRONT DOOR*

WRITTEN AND ILLUSTRATED BY
ZOPHIA MCDOUGAL

EMP Books
Kansas City, MO
www.EMPbooks.com

Copyright © 2017 by Zophia McDougal

All rights reserved. No part of this book may be reproduced, scanned, or distributed in any printed or electronic form, including information storage and retrieval systems, without permission. Please do not participate in or encourage piracy of copyrighted materials in violation of the author's rights. Please purchase only authorized editions.

First Edition: 11 7 5 3 2 1
ISBN: 978-0-9985077-5-0

This book is a work of fiction. Names, characters, places, dates, and incidents are products of the author's imagination, or are used fictitiously, satirically, or as parody. Any resemblance to actual persons, living or dead, business establishments, events, or locales is entirely coincidental.

LET'S GO WATCH THE BALL GAME
LET'S GET DRUNK AT THE BAR.
BUY ME SOME FRENCH FRIES AND A PITCHER OF BEER,
I DON'T CARE WHAT THE BARTENDER HEARS!
WE'LL ALL ROOT, ROOT, ROOT, FOR OUR FAVORITE MASCOT
IF THEY DON'T WIN WE WON'T CARE
FOR IT'S ONE, TWO, THREE SHOTS, WE'RE DRUNK
AND TOMORROW IS THE STATE FAIR.

One morning you awoke to a hissing noise. Through the main room of your small space, towards the window, was a the sunrise. The city is frosted and people are covered in thickets. You stand, following hissing noises with the same neck and eyes that were asleep moments ago. Your eyes grew large inside of drops from the melting frost. Thousands falling outside your window. Rainbows discovered inside each one and for a second, you were at a disco. Reporters had been talking about a desperate need for water in the valley but you only heard that part of the story. You gazed and your cheeks lifted. Light got lighter and you rushed through the back door, running to the sun, which was rising over the ledge that quarantined the valley that caused the water sprinkler to appear majestically crystal, dancing on your grounds which were long lost and taken from every drop that falls now.

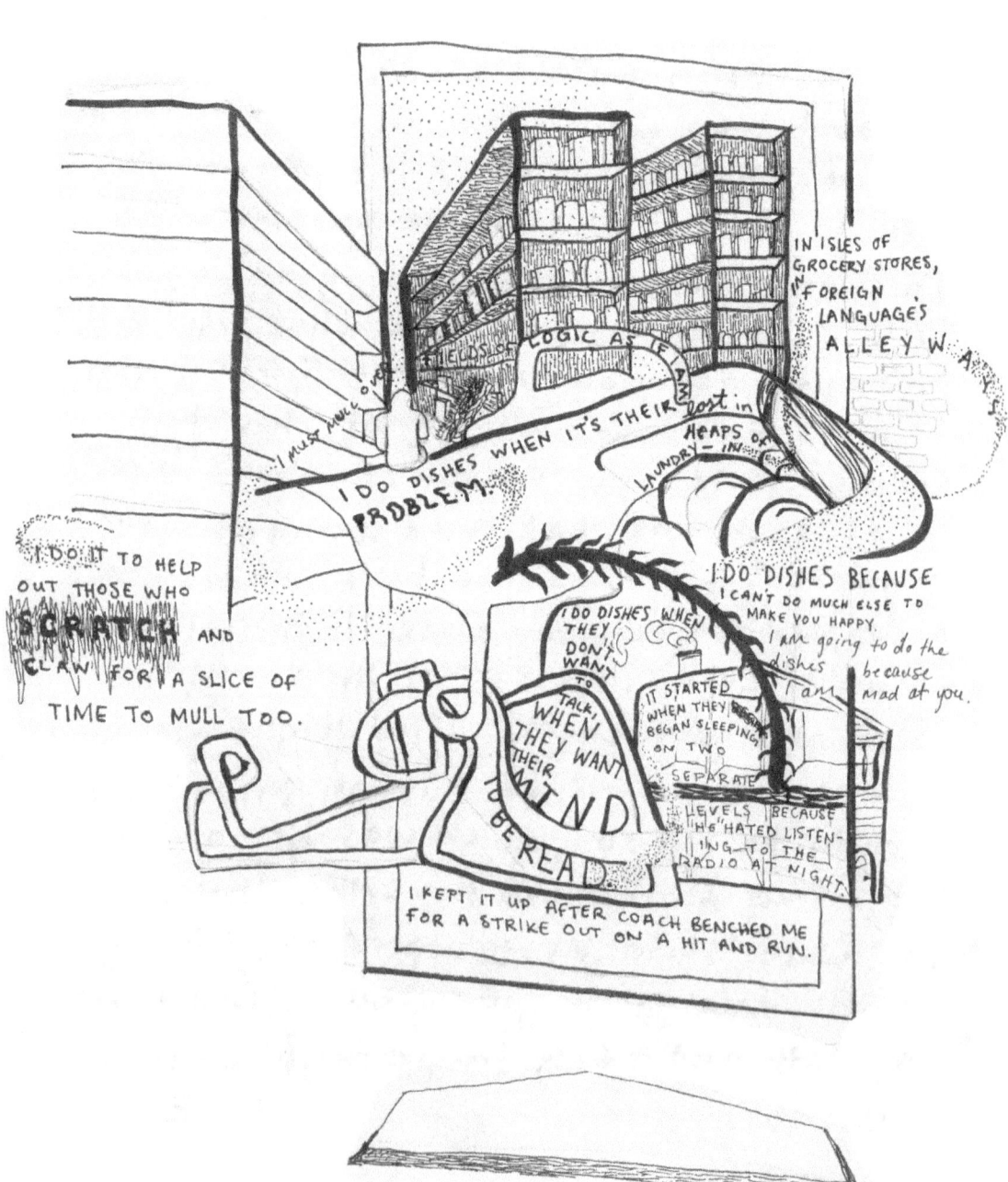

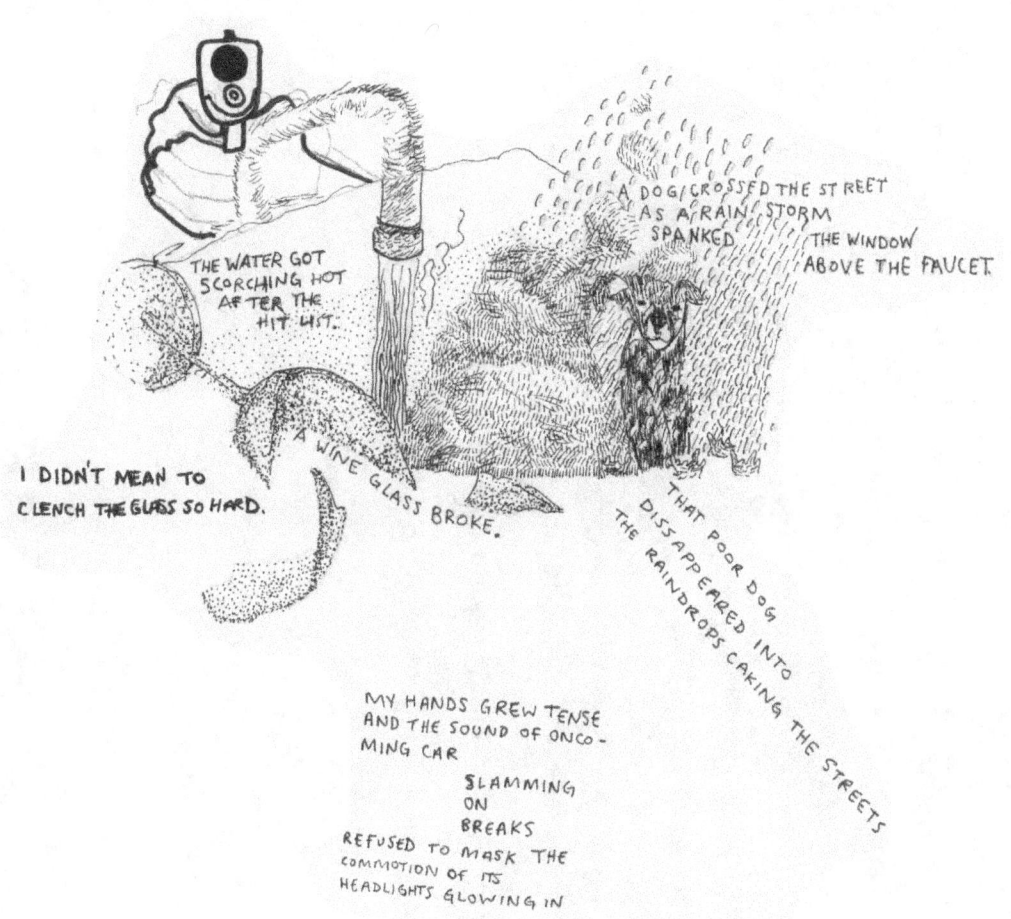

THEY SPIT THEIR NAILS.

THEY GRAB A PORTION OF THE NAILBED WHERE THEIR TEETH CAN GRIP.

THEY PULL UNTIL THEY TUG UNTIL THIN SLICES OF KERATIN RIP FALLING ONTO FAKE BAMBOO RUGS AND RUSTIC PICNIC TABLES.

EVEN
ANGELS
HAVE CRAVINGS
FOR NOTHING.

THEY'VE GOT NOTHING BETTER TO DO BUT PICK
IN THE BACKROOM.
NO ONE WILL SEE.

I HAVE TO MAKE INVENTORY OF THE UNIVERSE

I HAVE TO MAKE INVENTORY OF THE UNIVERSE

I HAVE TO MAKE INVENTORY OF THE UNIVERSE

I HAVE TO MAKE INVENTORY OF THE UNIVERSE

I need to be held
I'll go do that tonight.

A SPRINKLER FOLDS BACK AND FORTH IN THE AFTERNOON WATER, WITH A FLICK IN THE HEADS DIRECTION

BLANKETS TWENTY FEET OF 9% TOTAL CIRCUMFERENCE

I AM NOT FAR AWAY FROM YOU

1" ISN'T FAR FROM YOU green grass and yellow leaves cuddling in the palm of mother's dry hands and papa's arms wrapped around in the form of a cement curb

# THE BANG

ON HIM

They throw metal dumpsters on M and fill Him with the materials used to build what HE has longed for since the day he left himself to be the man he was supposed to be.

GREEN GRASS GROWS ON THE OTHER SIDE OF HIM AND MOTHER SCOFFS.

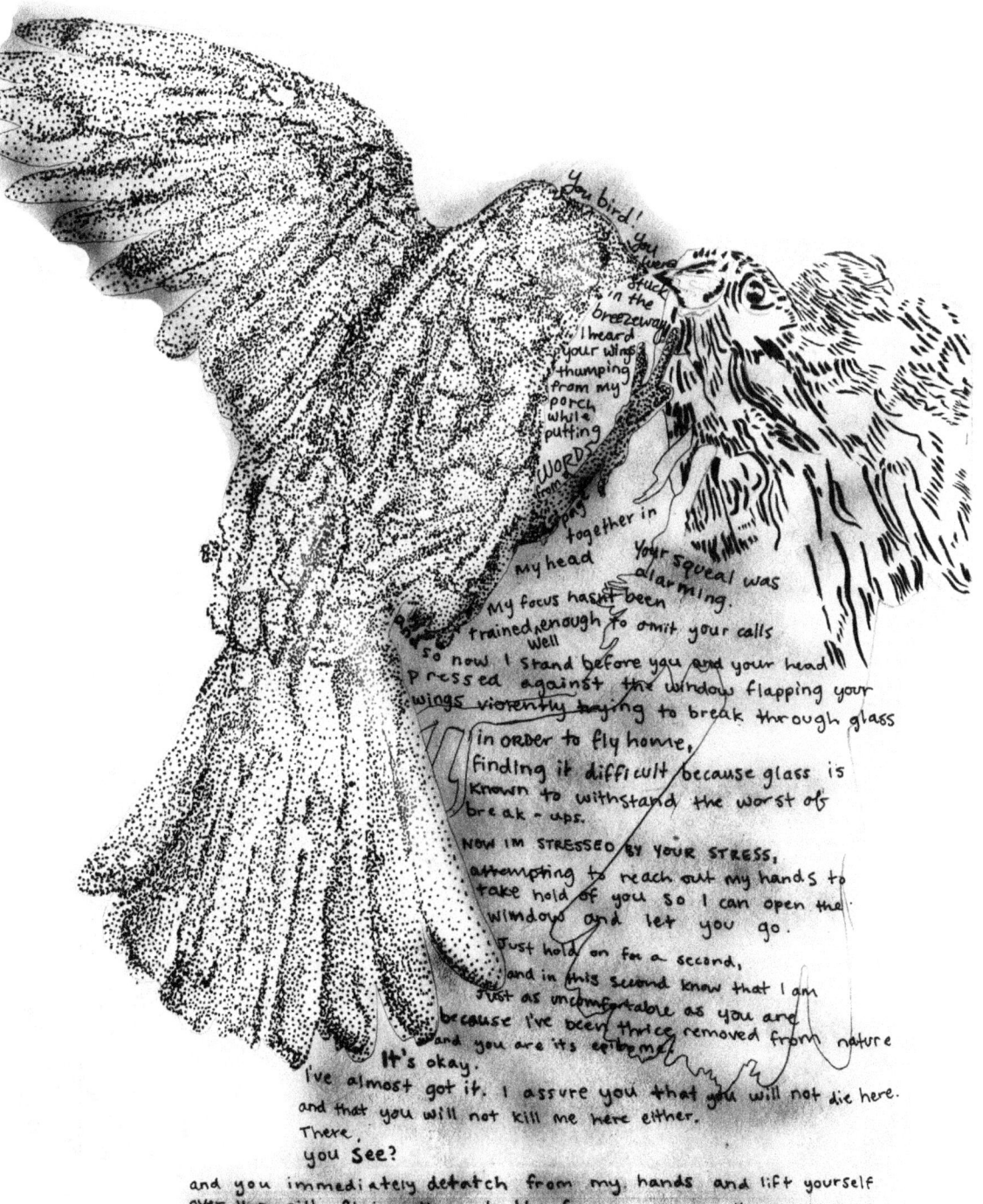

people say that I will one day. that one day someone will be as obsessed with me as I them. I'd rather them be as obsessed with themselves as much as I am with myself and, at the same time, let our obsessions push each other towards being better versions of what we originally were.

Can the space we create take a form that gets shit done? Can we work together, on ourselves?

I don't want to feel like im asking a lot of you. Like at any moment you will drop me from this cliff we've built using two pairs of hands alongside the help of hands that hold our arms up. Too many cliffs do that already and I don't want this to become unclimbable — a dust or a failed right angle.

In the attempt to be precise I must be honest about the time I ripped the paper crooked to where the image wasn't lined up correctly to the edge. We had to trim. It was mostly bullshit thrown at us from realities of concepts in the eateries while we were sinking into stools, drawing on walls, and bickering about our favorite cereal. I want to rest, assured that I'll never know you and trust you with my death all in the same while I learn how to listen so much to you that your words turn to sounds and your sounds turn to movements and your movements die and ressureet themselves as a new language. When we part into the world, I want our attempt at love to inspire both of our beings to love through lonelies and stubborns and naysays and disregards and absolutes.

Every single loophole contains a discovery next to an answer and nothing is okay. Okay is okay. I cannot read your handwriting because of how close each letter sits on top of its neighbor. You cannot read my mind because I have no words for it. But there's this belief in you in me, in me that I have in you. Eat a cheeseburger with onion rings. I'll make pierogies and asparagus. It's okay. Let me go when you're gone and tag me it when we're near. Be purple and treat yourself with the realest of golds. The big people tell us that it's not safe from the screen of our phones, but I want to go outside and you want to go to space.

please bring me to all of
the things
I have never touched.
More so
bring me
to the me
I've
never touched.

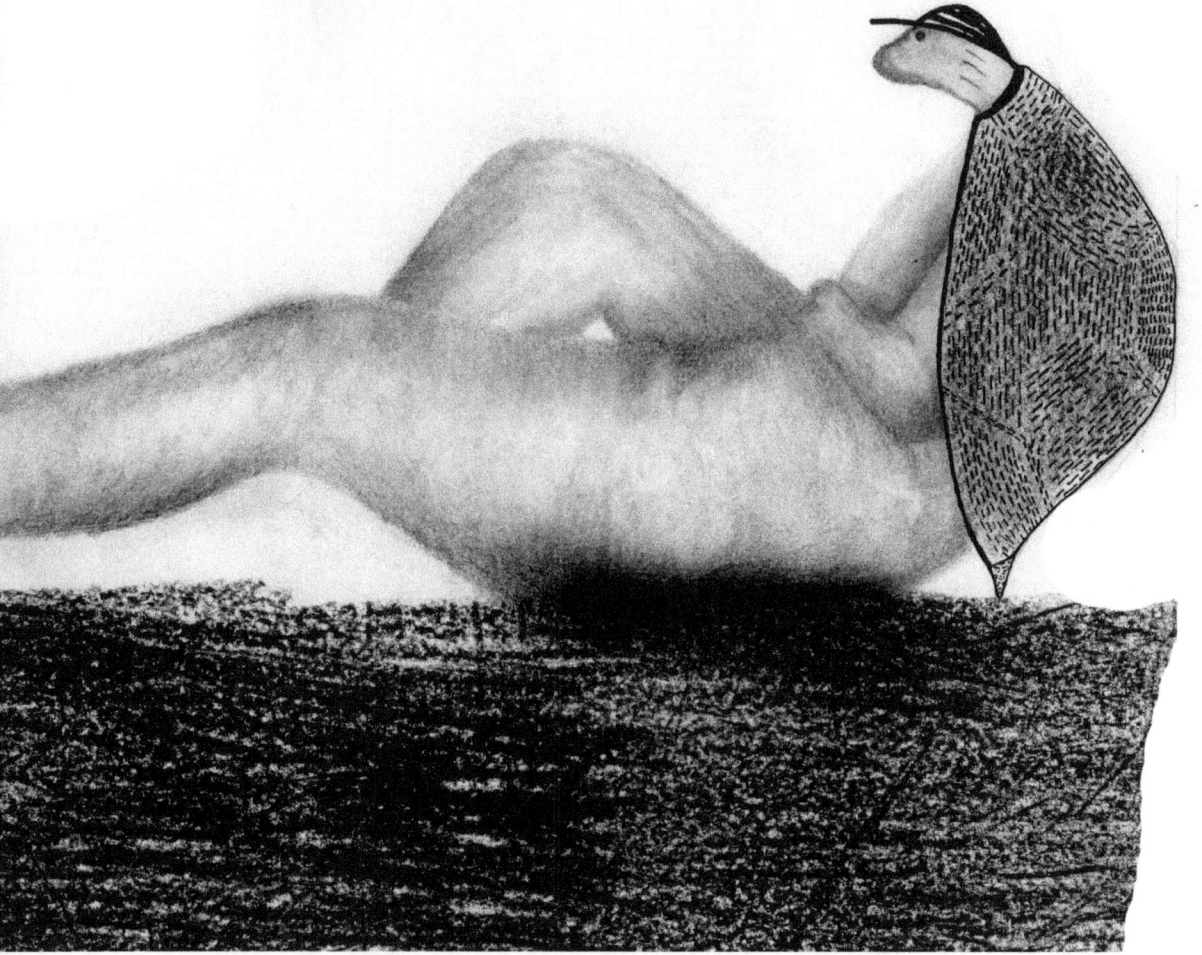

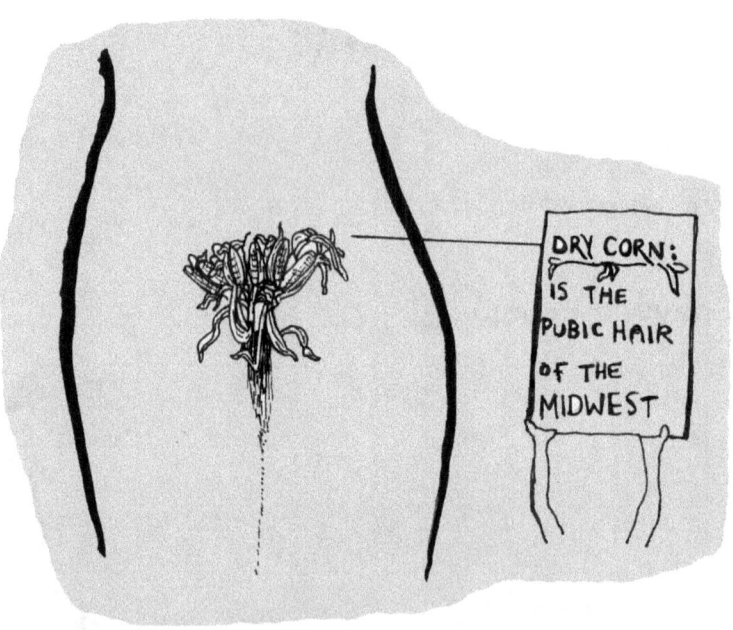

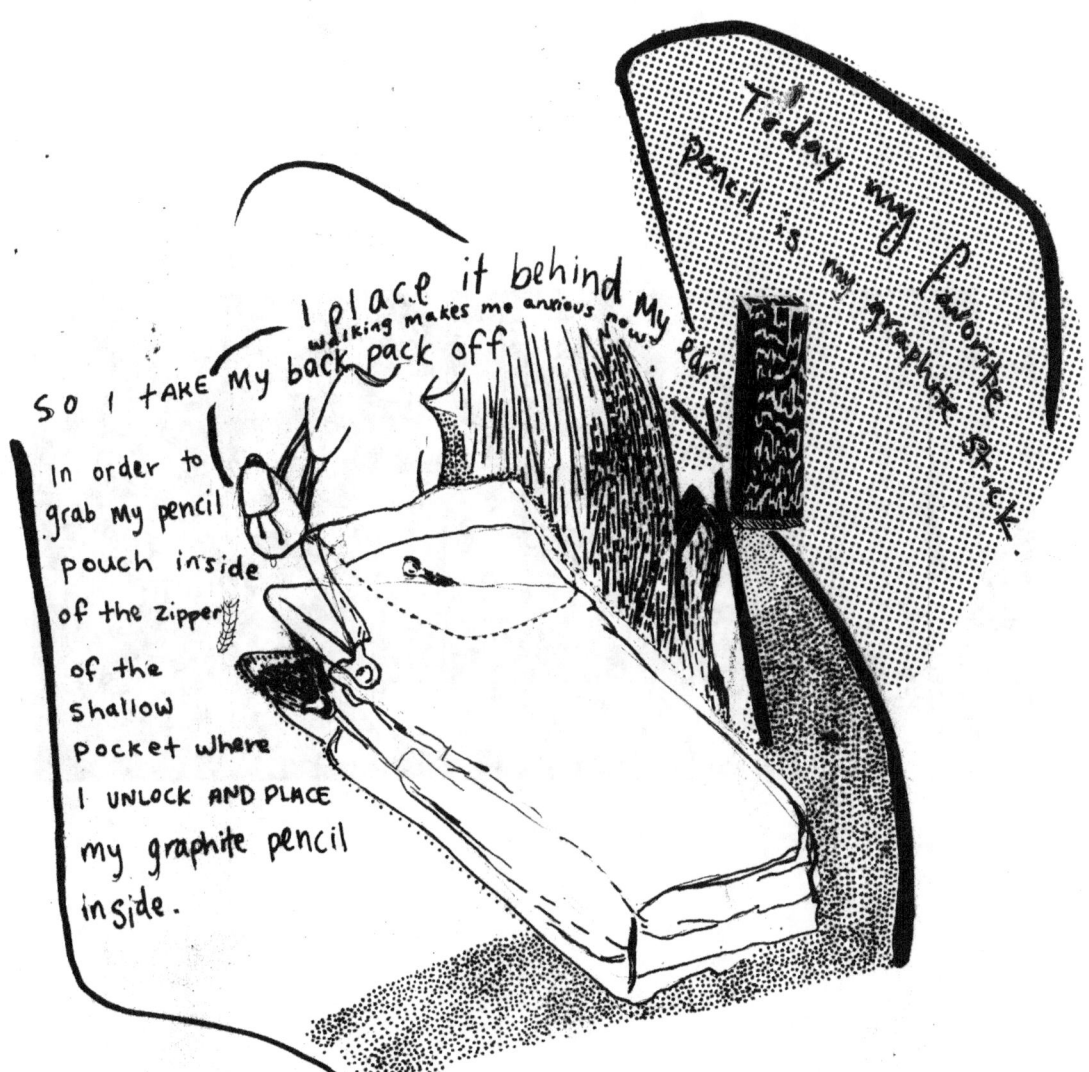

When they speak a scentence and they don't know what they said and they know you know that what they said wasn't what they really meant, but they said it and now it grows like vines, covering brick walls, crawling through windows, climbing onto the person looking outside, toward likeness, trying to find a way to land safely onto the ground after the fall.

when innocence isn't negotiated by fear ...

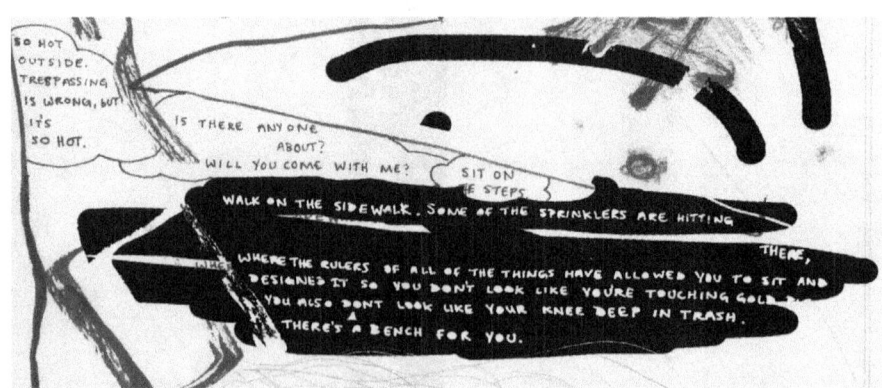

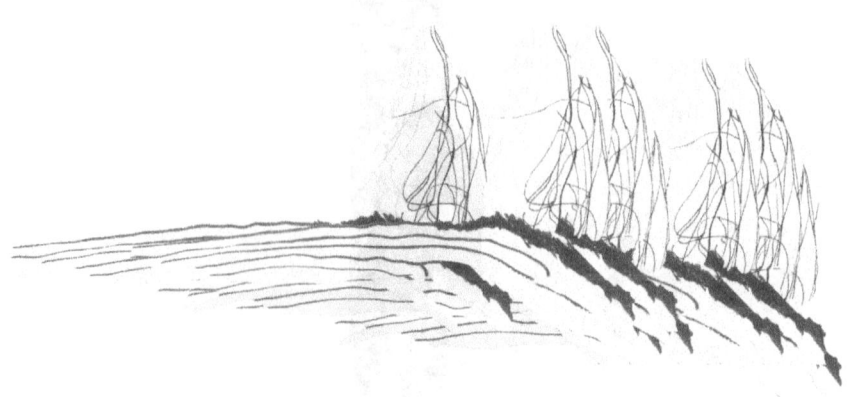

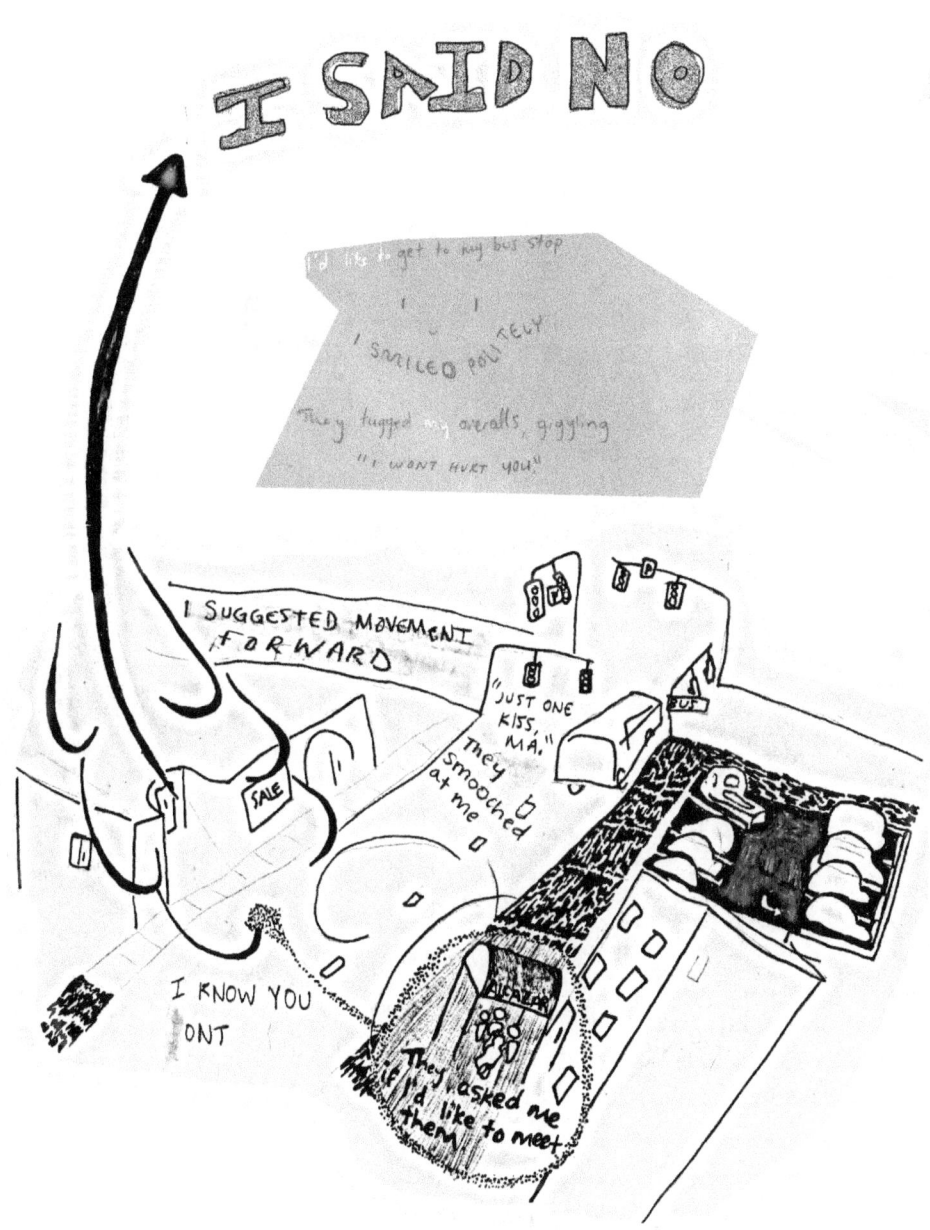

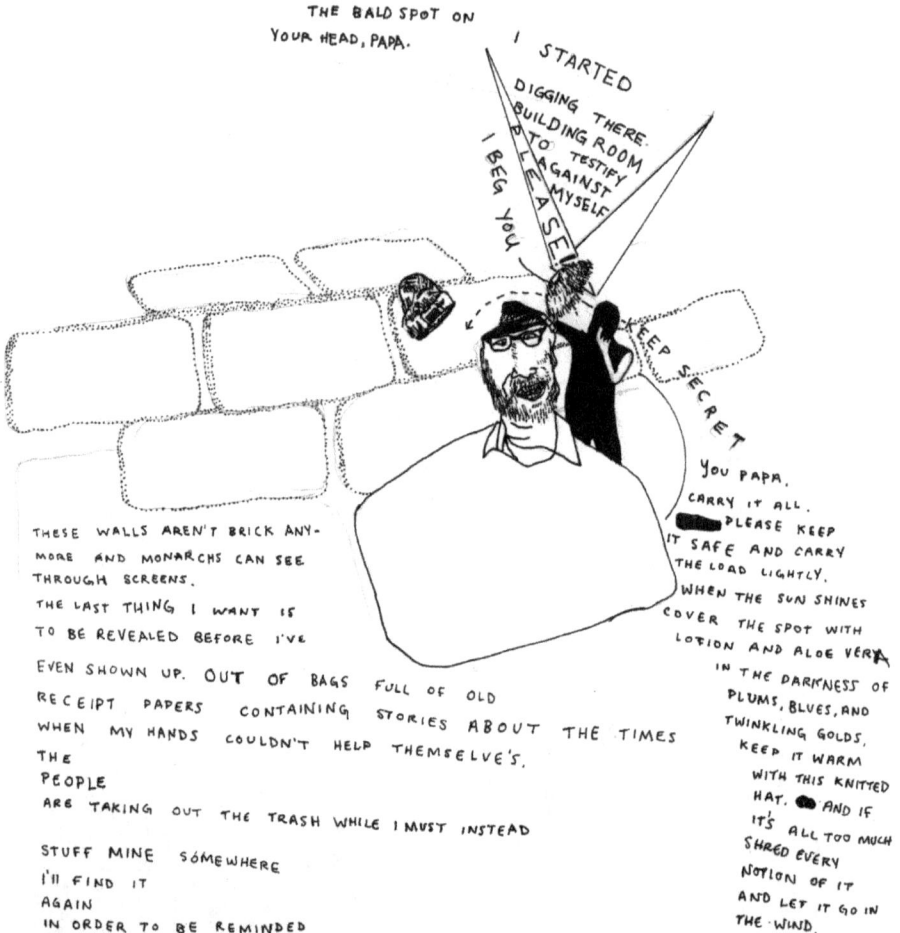

dear
bus driver,
if
you
count
how many times    you
              push
on the breaks
and
     multiply that by
the intesity




                of the smell

inside of your


    rolling    office

you will find
how
many
poems
you have been apart
of in order for
words
to
come
        alive.



Thanks a lot for the
ride home.


           Thanks a lot.

THESE WERE THE
MOVEMENTS
DEEMED UNINTERESTING
TO MIDTOWN OR
DOWNTOWN. THESE
WERE THE MOVEMENTS
OF ELOQUENT RAVAGES
COMMUNICATING WITH
JINGLING KEYS, MIX
TAPES, POSTURES, AND
EXCHANGES BETWEEN
EYES AND THEIR LIDS,
SLOWLY LIFTING AND
FALLING IN A MATTER OF
SECONDS IN ORDER TO
SEND A MESSAGE.

TWO LIONS SENDING
FLARES
ACROSS A BUS.

PASSENGERS PORTRAY
THEMSELVES AS TURTLES
INSIDE OF WINTER COATS.

CREEKS FREEZE AND
BIRDS FLY
TO CORNERS.

THE BEASTS INITIATE
CONTACT BETWEEN EACH
OTHER'S JOINTS.

A FALLEN MAMMOTH
CHANGES

THEIR PLAYLIST.

In the car you say it most of the time. When my face makes a face you say I'm sorry, but most of the time it isn't what you said it's how I take what you said and that's not a good reason to be sorry. Good in people get into fights with ugly all the time. There's no point in blaming. Keep towards the right unless you're not here because everything else is left handed and crooked. Let me call you honey after the bees are dead. Don't be so sorry because I like who you are even when it hurts. I have the right to leave at any point in time. As do you. I like to think we only have so many 'I'm sorry's before we spontaneously combust. Use them wisely because I want you around.

www.ingramcontent.com/pod-product-compliance
Lightning Source LLC
Chambersburg PA
CBHW060458300426
44113CB00016B/2641